D1466291

Now we know about...

GOOD MANNERS

Deborah Chancellor

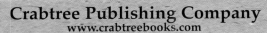

Crabtree Publishing Company
www.crabtreebooks.com

Published in Canada
Crabtree Publishing
616 Welland Avenue,
St. Catharines, Ontario
L2M 5V6

Published in the United States
Crabtree Publishing
PMB 16A,
350 Fifth Avenue, Suite 3308
New York, NY 10118

Editors: Belinda Weber, Lynn Peppas, Reagan Miller
Editorial director: Kathy Middleton
Production coordinator: Kenneth Wright
Prepress technician: Kenneth Wright
Studio manager: Sara Greasley
Designer: Trudi Webb
Production controller: Ed Green
Production manager: Suzy Kelly

Picture credits:
zoonar.com/Alamy: p. 18 (left)
Corbis: image100: p. 15 (bottom); Image Source: p. 17 (center left);
    Laurence Mouton/PhotoAlto: p. 22 (bottom left)
Getty Images: blue jean images: p. 16 (bottom left); Greg Ceo: p. 21 (bottom);
    ERproductions Ltd: p. 11 (top); Steve Gorton: p. 10 (bottom); Sean Justice:
    p. 4 (bottom); Andersen Ross: p. 11 (top); Bob Thomas: p. 11 (bottom)
iStock: front cover (bottom right), p. 8–9, 15 (top), 16 (top right), 19, 20, 23
Shutterstock: front cover (bottom left and top right), back cover (center right),
    p. 1, 4 (center), 5, 6, 7, 8 (bottom left), 9 (bottom), 10–11, 12–13, 14, 17 (bottom),
    18 (right), 21 (top), 22 (top right)

Every effort has been made to trace copyright holders, and we apologize in advance
for any omissions. We would be pleased to insert the appropriate acknowledgments
in any subsequent edition of this publication.

Library and Archives Canada Cataloguing in Publication

Chancellor, Deborah
    Good manners / Deborah Chancellor.

(Now we know about)
Includes index.
ISBN 978-0-7787-4719-2 (bound).--ISBN 978-0-7787-4736-9 (pbk.)

    1. Etiquette for children and teenagers--Juvenile literature.
2. Courtesy--Juvenile literature. 3. Respect--Juvenile literature.
I. Title. II. Series: Now we know about (St. Catharines, Ont.)

BJ1857.C5C43 2009   j395.1'22   C2009-903117-5

Library of Congress Cataloging-in-Publication Data

Chancellor, Deborah.
  Good manners / Deborah Chancellor.
    p. cm. -- (Now we know about)
  Includes index.
  ISBN 978-0-7787-4736-9 (pbk. : alk. paper) -- ISBN 978-0-7787-4719-2
(reinforced library binding : alk. paper)
 1. Courtesy--Juvenile literature. 2. Respect--Juvenile literature.
3. Children--Conduct of life. 4. Etiquette. I. Title. II. Series.

  BJ1533.C9C43 2009
  395.1'22--dc22

                                                    2009020920

Published in 2010 by Crabtree Publishing Company

Contents

The magic words

Good manners means you think of other people. You try not to upset them. You are careful about what you say. You are careful how you behave, too.

What should I say?

Always say "please" if you ask someone for something. Say "thank you" if someone has said or done something nice for you. These "magic words" will make people like you even more.

How can I thank people?

Remember to thank people when they are kind to you. You can call the person on the phone to say thank you, if he or she is not with you.

Talking Point

Why is it important to say please and thank you?

Say please and thank you to people. It shows you know that they are doing something for you. It tells others you are thankful for their help.

Write it down!

You can send thank you letters, texts, or emails. This is a way of showing you are **grateful**.

writing thank you notes

5

Having a chat

Sometimes it is hard to talk to people if you are **shy**. But if people ask you questions you should answer. Always look at people when you talk to them, too.

Are you listening?

Listen carefully when you talk to your friends. Look at them when they are talking. This shows you are paying attention to what they are saying.

Let your friend finish speaking before you say something.

If you do not hear what someone says to you, say "pardon?" Do not ask "what?" Pardon is more **polite**.

6

Are you bored?

Show you are interested by asking people questions. Do not forget to listen to their answers. If you do not listen, you might ask them about something they have already told you.

Talking Point

Why is it important to listen when you are having a conversation?

Give people time to tell you what they want to say. Listening shows that you **respect** how they feel about something. You might even learn something new.

How do I stay cool?

It is hard to remember your manners if you lose your **temper**. Even if you are very angry with something that has been said or done, do not shout. People will listen more if you keep your voice down and speak calmly.

Can I speak now?

Do not **interrupt** a person when they are talking. Wait until they have finished speaking. Then it is your turn to talk.

Can you hear me?

It is bad manners to shout or stamp your feet. Even if you know you are right, do not do it.

Let people finish talking, even if you do not think what they are saying is right.

Talking point

What happens when you lose your temper?

When you are angry it is easy to upset someone else. This might get you into trouble. You might say something you are sorry about later. Try to listen to what the other person is saying.

Watch your language

Do not **swear** or use words that you know are **rude**. Speak to others as you would like them to speak to you.

I am sorry

Always remember to say sorry if you hurt someone. Say sorry if you broke something that belongs to them. It does not matter if it was an accident. It is still important to say sorry so the person knows you feel badly for making them feel unhappy.

Forgive and forget

If someone says sorry to you accept their **apology**. Do not remind them later about what they did.

Are you sorry?

Show someone you are sorry by doing something nice for them. You might give them a hug or some flowers.

What are you waiting for?

It is never too late to say you are sorry. But it is better to apologize right away. You do not want things to get worse between you and the other person.

TalKing PoiNt

Why is it important to say sorry?

Saying sorry shows that you really wish you had not done, or said, anything that hurt someone else. This may help the person you upset forgive you. You can become friends again.

Try to show that you are sorry for what you did.

WORD WIZARD!
apologize
When you apologize to someone, you are saying that you are sorry for what you did.

11

How do I show respect?

Showing someone respect means you look up to them. You treat them as you would want to be treated.

Is that fair?

It is bad manners to push into a line. Other people may have been waiting in line for a long time.

Are you sick?

People do not want your germs. Cover your mouth with a tissue when you cough or sneeze. Put your hand over your mouth when you yawn.

Use a tissue to catch any germs when you sneeze.

What is the hurry?

When you go through a door, hold it open for the people behind you. It is the polite thing to do!

Remember to thank people if they hold a door open for you.

Talking point

What does it mean to show someone respect?

Showing someone respect means you care about the way you treat them. You care about what they think of you. Treat people kindly. It shows you think about what they need too.

Staying safe

It is important to listen to what adults say. They might be telling you something important. They might say something that will keep you safe.

Show respect to everyone, not just your friends.

13

Be thoughtful

You share your home with your family. Be **thoughtful** toward the people you live with. Do not wait for them to do everything for you. Try to do things that you can do for yourself. Try to be helpful.

Keep it clean

Help keep the bathroom tidy. Hang up towels. Put your toothbrush back where it belongs.

14

Have you finished?

Try to leave things as tidy as you found them. Be considerate when you use the toilet. Remember that others have to use it after you!

Always flush the toilet. Leave the seat down after you have used it.

Can you help?

When you come home, wipe your shoes on a mat. Take them off if you are asked to. Do not leave your shoes lying around by the door. Make sure you put them away.

Your clothes and shoes may be dirty if you have been playing outside.

Talking point

What does being considerate mean?

Being considerate means you are thinking about the feelings of other people. It shows you are not just thinking about yourself. Being considerate means you are trying to understand how someone else might feel.

15

What is a good welcome?

It is polite to give a good **welcome** to family and friends who visit your home. Stop what you are doing. Get up and say hello to your **guests**.

Try to make visitors feel welcome in your home.

How are you?

Make your guests feel at home by talking to them. Ask them questions. You could show them something special, such as your favorite toy.

Would you like to sit down?

When visitors come, do not **ignore** them or go away. If there are a lot of visitors in your home, give up your seat. Let them sit down so they feel comfortable.

Stay and talk to your guests to show that you are pleased to see them.

Talking Point

Why is it important to say hello and goodbye?

People think you are happy to see them when you say hello. Remember to say goodbye too. People might think that you did not like seeing them if you do not.

a remote control

What do you want to watch?

If you are watching TV and guests come into the room, ask them if they would like to change the channel. They might even want to turn the TV off so they can talk to you.

Time to eat

Meals are a good time for people to sit down and talk. They are also a good time to remember your manners!

Use a napkin to wipe your mouth.

Dinner is ready!

Always come to a meal when you are called. Wait until everyone is served before you start eating.

Are you a messy eater?

Move your chair close to the table. This way you will not drop food on the floor.

Do I have to eat it?

If you do not like something you are served, leave it on the side of your plate. Do not **complain**. Stay at the table until everyone is done eating.

Remember to thank the cook after a meal.

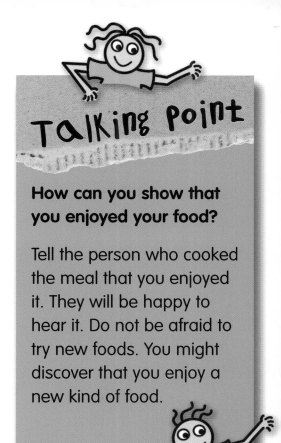

Talking Point

How can you show that you enjoyed your food?

Tell the person who cooked the meal that you enjoyed it. They will be happy to hear it. Do not be afraid to try new foods. You might discover that you enjoy a new kind of food.

WORD WIZARD!
served

If you are served a meal, it means that someone gives you food to eat, usually at a table.

Table manners

Good table manners mean you eat politely. You behave well at meal times. Table manners help keep everyone happy!

Are you hungry?

Remember to chew your food with your mouth closed. Do not talk while you chew. Try not to eat too quickly—even if it is delicious and you are really hungry.

When you eat with a knife and fork, hold food with your fork and cut it with your knife.

Please could you pass that?

Do not stretch across the table if you cannot reach something. Ask someone to pass you what you need.

Talking Point

Does it matter how you eat your food?

Yes it does! Other people do not want to see you stuff food into your mouth, or chew with your mouth open. It might make them not want their meal. Remember to swallow your food before you take another bite.

Can I play?

Do not read or play video games at the dinner table. It is also rude to make phone calls or send texts while people are eating.

video game

21

Around the world

Around the world different cultures have different manners. What is polite in one place might be rude in another.

Is it polite?

In India, it shows good manners to leave a small amount of food on your plate. This shows that you have had enough to eat.

Why do they do that?

In some countries people kiss each other on the cheek when they say hello and goodbye. In other countries people shake hands when they meet.

Was that you?

Some things are rude wherever you go. You may think rude noises are funny, but other people may not think so.

It is polite to say "pardon me" if you make rude noises in front of other people.

Talking Point

Why are manners different around the world?

People of different cultures may think that different things are rude. It is important to respect the culture that you are in. Listen to what adults tell you about the **customs** and **traditions** of places you visit. You do not want to upset people by mistake.

Glossary

apology Saying you are sorry for something

complaining Moaning or grumbling about something

custom The way things are usually done

grateful Feeling happy that something has happened

guests Visitors to your home

ignore Take no notice of something

interrupt Stop somebody from talking

polite Showing good manners

respect Treat someone thoughtfully

rude Not being polite or showing bad manners to people

shy Feeling embarrassed or scared of people at events

swear To use rude language or gestures to upset other people

temper A person's mood or feelings toward something

thoughtful Thinking about what other people would like, and putting other people's feelings first

traditions Things that have been done in the same way for a long time. These may be different in other countries or places

welcome Showing that you are happy when somebody comes over

Index

Printed In the U.S.A.- CG